ODD ANIMAL HELPERS

by Gabrielle Reyes

SCHOLASTIC INC.

New York   Toronto London   Auckland
Sydney   Mexico City   New Delhi   Hong Kong

Photo credits
Front Cover (clockwise): © Ann & Steve Toon/Robert Harding Library/Alamy,
© MartinMaritz/Shutterstock, © James A Dawson/Shutterstock; Back cover:
© Tammy Peluso/Oxford Scientific/Getty Images

Interior: Page 3: © Chris Fourie/Shutterstock, © ETIENjones/Shutterstock; Pages 4-5:
© Ben Cranke (RF)/Getty Images, © DM Gordon/Shutterstock; Pages 6-7: © James A
Dawson/Shutterstock, © George Toubalis/Shutterstock; Pages 8-9: © Rand McMeins (RF)/
Getty Images, © SeDmi/Shutterstock; Pages 10-11: © David Mckee/Shutterstock,
© littlesam/Shutterstock; Pages 12-13: © John A. Anderson/Shutterstock, © norhazlan/
Shutterstock; Page 14: © Ewan Chesser/Shutterstock; Page 15: © FLPA /Alamy;
Pages 16-17: © Kirsanov/Shutterstock, © somchaij/Shutterstock; Pages 18-19: © Oxford
Scientific/Getty Images; Pages 20-21: © David Fleetham/Visuals Unlimited, Inc/Getty
Images, © Mauro Rodrigues/Shutterstock; Pages 22-23: © Steve Ralston/iStock Photo,
© Phoric/Shutterstock; Page 24: © robbosphotos/Shutterstock; Page 25: © MartinMaritz/
Shutterstock, © Pan Xunbin/Shutterstock; Page 26-27: © James Knighten/iStockphoto,
© Beata Becla/Shutterstock; Pages 28-29: © Chad Graham (RF)/Getty Images, © Pan Xun-
bin/Shutterstock; Pages 30-31: © Ben Cranke (RF)/Getty Images,
© DM Gordon/Shutterstock

Animals often survive in unexpected ways. Sometimes even big animals like the rhinoceros need a little help. When an animal pairs up with a different kind of animal or plant for help, it is called a *symbiotic relationship*. Every day, countless animals work together in unique ways.

PERFECT PARTNERS

Oxpeckers are birds that survive by helping bigger animals, such as rhinoceroses, hippos, **zebras**, and oxen. The small birds eat blood-sucking insects. The birds get a filling meal and in return, their big friends don't get sick from bug bites!

Getting Fishy

Symbiotic relationships are everywhere— even under the sea! On coral reefs, **cleaner shrimp** lay in wait. When a **moray eel** comes swimming by, the shrimp hops on for a snack. The shrimp eats leftover food around the eel's mouth. It also eats pests and dead skin that could make the eel sick.

This big **tiger grouper** doesn't scare tiny **cleaner gobies**. They'll swim right into the grouper's mouth!

Fearless Fish

While the gobies get a good meal of food from inside and around the fish's mouth, the tiger grouper gets nice and clean.

CLOWNING

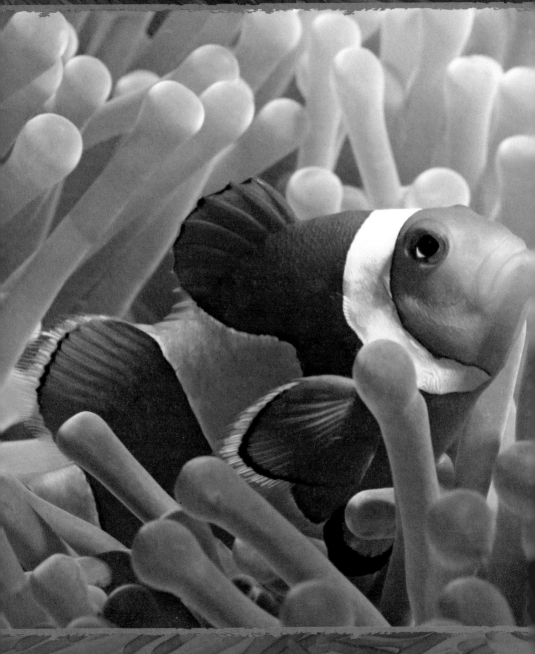

AROUND

It may look like the **clownfish** is swimming in the leaves of a sea plant. But those are actually the stinging tentacles of a **sea anemone**. Clownfish are coated in slimy *mucus* that protects them against the sea anemone's painful stings. Other fish aren't so lucky. A clownfish can lure big, hungry fish into the sea anemone's stinging tentacles—and its hidden mouth! The anemone gets the main meal and the clownfish gets the leftovers.

CREATURE CAMOUFLAGE

Decorator crabs avoid being attacked by *predators* by attaching **sponges** and other sea creatures to their shells. The crabs are left alone by their enemies to find food in peace while the sea creatures get transported from one place to another.

Sweet Treat

The honeyguide bird and the ratel, which is also known as the honey badger, are a good team. The honeyguide bird flies around looking for beehives. When it finds one, it calls out. The honey badger comes running and gets to work. Its tough, furry skin protects it from bee stings while it breaks into the hive. When the badger is done eating what it wants, the honeyguide bird swoops in and eats the rest!

Bug Off!

Aphids are tiny insects that live on plants. They suck the juice out of plants and produce a waste called honeydew. Honeydew is the perfect food for hungry **ants**. To protect their food source, ants will defend aphids against any insects that try to harm them. Some ants even help protect aphid eggs over the winter.

Bug Buddies

Sometimes animals pair up but only one partner benefits. The **pseudoscorpion** is a spiderlike creature that is so small it can ride on insects. Not only does it get free transportation, but it gets the protection of the bigger bug.

Go Fish

Remora fish have special dorsal fins that act as suction cups. They attach themselves to animals such as sharks, **turtles**, manta rays, and dugongs for an easy ride.

When the bigger animal hunts its *prey*, the remora eats whatever is left over. While the big animals don't gain anything from the remora fish, they don't seem to mind the company.

Hitch a Ride

Barnacles are sea creatures that can't move around on their own. They attach to big ocean animals, such as whales that will move around for them. Then the barnacles can use their long, feathery appendages to skim the water for tiny organisms to eat.

Bird BRAIN

Birds may have small brains, but that doesn't mean they're not smart. In Africa, egrets spend time with animals such as rhinoceroses and hippos. When the big animals walk through the savannahs, they stir up tiny creatures on the ground. The egrets are right there waiting to gobble them up.

FLOWER POWER

Sometimes even plants and animals can help each other out. Plants survive by producing seeds from which new plants can grow. A **bee** can help **flowering plants** make seeds. When the insect drinks nectar from a flower, it gets covered in *pollen*. When the bee flies to another flower, it spreads the pollen. That flower uses the pollen to make new seeds.

Winging It

While bees like to land on flowers to eat, **hummingbirds** hover in the air during a meal. With their long beaks, hummingbirds are able to help **flowers** with special shapes make new seeds.

Friends Forever

Every day, nature is hard at work—from the
most delicate flower to the most agile impala.
Whether animals fly in the sky, run in the
grass, or swim in the sea, they help each
other in surprising ways.

GLOSSARY:

Mucus: A thick, slimy liquid

Organism: A living thing, such as a plant or animal

Pollen: Tiny yellow grains produced and used by flowers for reproduction

Predator: An animal that lives by hunting other animals for food

Prey: An animal that is hunted by other animals for food

Symbiotic relationship: A relationship between two organisms in which at least one benefits from the other